Original title:
The Mighty Madrone

Copyright © 2025 Creative Arts Management OÜ
All rights reserved.

Author: Lucas Harrington
ISBN HARDBACK: 978-1-80567-286-9
ISBN PAPERBACK: 978-1-80567-585-3

Harmony in Diversity

In the forest, all must agree,
A squirrel wears a hat, oh, what a spree!
The owl hoots tunes in the late night glow,
While raccoons dance, putting on quite the show.

With colors so bright, trees wear a fit,
A mushroom on a branch, never one to quit!
Together they sing, a whimsical band,
Nature's wild party, oh, isn't it grand?

Reflections of the Dawn

Dawn breaks with laughter, the sun's a wisecrack,
Rays tickle the earth, no talent they lack.
Bugs belt out tunes as they flit to and fro,
While the brook giggles softly, ensuring the flow.

Bees in bow ties, they buzz at their ease,
Cheeky little critters, always aiming to please.
The morning's parade, with humor in bloom,
Nature's own circus, it lights up the gloom.

Guardian of the Grove

A tree stands tall, a sentinel wise,
With branches like arms, reaching for the skies.
It chuckles at pine cones, diving with flair,
And whispers to geese that float in the air.

To watch over the forest, it takes a deep breath,
With roots like a jester, it avoids all death.
It sways with the winds, dancing a jig,
As the fox stops to look, thinking, 'What a big twig!'

Whispering Canopy

Underneath green roofs, there's giggles galore,
With shadows that wiggle, and leaves that adore.
The branches engage in a light-hearted chat,
While the sun peeks through, playing hide and pat.

Each rustle a riddle, each drop a delight,
As critters perform in the soft, dappled light.
The canopy whispers, 'Join in the cheer!'
Nature's amusing tales, for all who come near.

Telling Tales of Tomorrow

In a forest where whispers play,
The trees gossip all day.
One says it will rain pies,
While another rolls its eyes.

Little squirrels in their hats,
Debate the best cheese for gnats.
Raccoons throw a wild dance,
While the owls give a glance.

Knots in trunks, a signage spree,
Telling tales for you and me.
The ferns chuckle at the jokes,
As the mushrooms share their pokes.

So come and join the leafy jest,
In their leafy, laughing fest.
Tomorrow's tales will make you grin,
From the tallest bark to the thinnest pin.

Archway of the Ancients

Beneath a leafy, twisted frame,
Ancient trees play a funny game.
Telling stories of the past,
With giggles that come fast.

Lizards race on mossy ground,
While wise old toads make no sound.
Every branch, a curious glee,
As the air sings with esprit.

A squirrel in a flowery dent,
Wears a cap—dapper and bent.
He winks and beckons you near,
To show you where they've stored the beer.

Underneath this ancient yawn,
Fables flow like the dawn.
Step through mist, take a chance,
Experience the forest's dance.

Pillar of Solitude

In a clearing, solitary flair,
Stands a tree without a care.
With a chuckle, it shares its plight,
"Who needs pals on a quiet night?"

Foxes prance, but it just leans,
Rooted deep, where laughter greens.
"I tell my jokes to passing winds,
For lonely whispers are good friends."

Sunsets blush with a cheeky grin,
While starlings play their violin.
Its branches sway without a fuss,
As it laughs, "No need for us!"

So here it stands, a comic soul,
Absorbing every silvery shoal.
Pillar of solitude, wise and spry,
Making merry with the sky.

Journals of the Journey

Leaves rustle like turning pages,
Each an entry that engages.
A journal kept by nature's hand,
Filled with giggles from the land.

Ducks quack of their latest quests,
Bouncing on the lily's crests.
While wind chuckles at its tales,
Playing tricks and raising sails.

Crickets chirp their nightly thoughts,
In the pot of nature's pots.
Every critter joins the fun,
As moonlight listens, one by one.

So flip through pages of the green,
And find the stories, bright and keen.
In journals where the laughter's free,
Nature writes its history.

Secrets in the Bark

In the wood, a story hides,
Tales of squirrels and their rides.
With each knot, a giggle waits,
As birds debate their dinner plates.

Cracks and crevices, a joke or two,
A secret shared just between the crew.
Chipmunks whisper from the shade,
While the breeze joins in the charade.

Hollow hearts of wooden smiles,
Laughing leaves for miles and miles.
Underneath the canopy's cover,
Nature's punchlines, like no other.

So if you stop and take a look,
You'll find the fun in every nook.
With a smile, the forest shall speak,
In barky rhymes, it's never bleak.

Resilience in Bloom

A flower poked through cracks with flair,
Winking at the world, without a care.
It danced in rain and thrived in dirt,
With laughter that could never hurt.

When storms would brew, it just stood still,
Swaying gently, a flower will.
"Who needs sun?" it chimed with glee,
"I've got raindrops just for me!"

It wore a crown of dazzling bees,
Buzzing laughter in the breeze.
Every petal, a happy tune,
Waving brightly to the moon.

So here's to blooms that jest and play,
In every color, bright and gay.
Resilience wrapped in petals tight,
A funny bloom, a pure delight.

Sentinel of the Forest

Standing tall, with a knowing grin,
Watching mischief with a spin.
The wise old tree with arms spread wide,
Chortling at the critters' ride.

Its branches sway as if to say,
"Hey, little fox, don't run away!"
Hooting owls join in the fun,
While bunnies race, they've just begun.

As squirrels plot their daring heists,
Sentinel chuckles, oh, how nice!
"Don't steal my acorns, that's a must,
I'll tickle you with leaves if you trust!"

So here he stands, the forest's jester,
In leafy robes, the ultimate tester.
With roots like stories, deep and wide,
A true friend rests by nature's side.

Roots of Ancient Wisdom

Beneath the soil, the whispers flow,
Guiding seedlings, in a row.
"Don't rush," they say, "just take your time,
Growing slow can be sublime."

With tangled tales of olden days,
The roots chuckle in their ways.
"Just look at us, we're wise and bold,
In clumpy earth, our laughter's told!"

They share the secrets, one by one,
The art of life, under the sun.
"Share your acorns, here's our plan,
A forest full of friends, not just a clan!"

So if you tread on leafy ground,
Listen close to the giggles found.
For in the roots, magic brews,
Ancient wisdom with a touch of muse.

Threads of the Green

In the forest, they prance and play,
Silly squirrels with nuts on display.
They chatter and dance up high,
While branches sway, oh my, oh my!

The leaves wear hats, oh what a sight,
Breeze whispers jokes, oh so light.
Frogs croak in rhythms, a croaky cheer,
Nature's comedy, loud and clear!

Beneath the arch of emerald hue,
A deer strikes a pose, thinks he's cute too.
Caterpillars do a wiggly dance,
While the sun shines down, a golden romance!

Each twig a tale, each root a laugh,
Giggling grasshoppers craft their own path.
In this green world, whimsy blooms,
Nature's humor forever looms!

Lullabies in the Leaves

As twilight falls, the night grips tight,
Crickets sing songs under pale moonlight.
The owls hoot softly, tales to tell,
While fireflies waltz like a fairy spell!

Leaves rustle whispers of dreams unfurled,
Each branch a cradle in a sleepy world.
Dancing shadows play peek-a-boo,
With the stars above, twinkling brightly too!

Bats swoop low, with a giggling chase,
While sleepy bears find their cozy space.
In this lullaby, the forest hums,
A symphony of snores, oh, here it comes!

So close your eyes, let dreams take flight,
In the arms of the woods, all feels right.
With soft wooden hugs and moonlit beams,
The night dances on in whimsical dreams!

Guardians of the Glade

In the glade, where laughter grows,
Mushrooms wear shoes, and sunlight glows.
Rabbits sworn in a royal decree,
Declare funniness their loyalty!

Badgers in capes, oh, what a sight,
Holding court, they rule the night.
With wisecracks and winks, they stand tall,
Keeping watch for the goofiest of all!

The brook babbles jokes, quite absurd,
Fish splash about, chirping a word.
In this haven where chuckles flow,
The guardians cheer, they steal the show!

Together they giggle, the trees shake their leaves,
This joyful brigade, no one deceives.
In the heart of the glade, hilarity sways,
Where laughter and joy fill up the days!

Realm of the Woodland Spirits

In realms where mischief flits about,
Pixies giggle, a little shout.
They sprinkle laughter like golden dust,
Building castles, a whimsical trust!

Gnomes in a race, oh speed demons wild,
With candy canes, they're utterly beguiled.
Their jolly dance leaves a trail of cheer,
As the trees sway low, embracing near!

Mice play chess with acorn caps,
While rabbits consider the best of naps.
Squirrels toast with acorn goblets high,
Toasting to joy as the day flutters by!

So join in the fun, let laughter ignite,
In this realm where spirits take flight.
With every giggle, a magic weave,
In the woodland bliss, it's hard to believe!

Flames and Feathers

In a forest where shadows play,
A tree dressed in colors that sway.
It tickles the clouds with its flair,
Whispering secrets to the air.

Its limbs do the cha-cha and twist,
While squirrels in tuxedos insist,
To join every dance through the night,
Under a moon that shines oh so bright.

Branches wear hats, and leaves have fun,
Making a racket beneath the sun.
With each gust of wind, they all cheer,
Creating a symphony we can hear!

So gather, my friends, let's join the spree,
For this treetop party is wild and free.
Flames of laughter ignited within,
In a woodland dance, let the fun begin!

Canopy Compositions

A grand orchestra high in the trees,
With woodpeckers drumming as they please.
A maestro perched near the tip-top,
Conducting the laughter that never will stop.

Each rustling leaf plays a note so sweet,
As critters in bow ties tap their feet.
The sunlight shines down like a spotlight,
Turning each branch into pure delight.

A raccoon sings opera out loud,
While a fox juggles sticks, feeling proud.
And everyone giggles at their own fun,
In this canopy where magic is spun.

With music and joy as the highest score,
We'll dance till the stars ask for more.
Every branch sways to this whimsical tune,
As twilight turns into a joyful June.

Spirits Among the Branches

Up in the branches, the spirits glide,
With eyes full of mischief and laughter wide.
They play tricks on squirrels, give them a scare,
As nuts rain down from high in the air.

With giggles echoing the evening song,
These cheeky ghosts never get it wrong.
They swing from the twigs, a mischievous crew,
Causing mayhem as they swoop and flew.

But do not fear these playful sprites,
For they throw dazzling, sparkly lights.
In every rustle and every swoosh,
Is a comedy show—their perfect hoosh.

So if you wander beneath their domain,
Just know you'll be part of their fun little game.
In the realm of the branches, let laughter arise,
With spirits as jesters in the night skies!

Dancers in the Twilight

As twilight falls, the dancers arrive,
With twirls and spins, they come alive.
A band of raccoons with style supreme,
Shaking their tails, living the dream.

Leaves flutter by like confetti in flight,
While fireflies join in, twinkling bright.
They wiggle and giggle in shadowy light,
Creating a scene that feels just right.

A rabbit in sneakers does the moonwalk,
While owls shout "Woohoo!" and chatty birds squawk.
The bark acts like a stage for this crew,
Where every spin makes the forest anew.

So come one, come all, to this shindig tonight,
Where creatures of nature dance with delight.
With laughter and joy that knows no end,
In the heart of the woods, let's all transcend!

Canopy Dreams

Up above, a squirrel spins,
Chasing dreams of acorn wins.
Leaves all giggle, branches sway,
In the sun, they dance and play.

Raccoons plot their midnight feasts,\nWhile owls joke like furry beasts.
They swap tall tales of old and wise,
Underneath the bright blue skies.

The sunlight tickles, shadows stretch,
Bouncing jokes like a game of fetch.
The breeze carries laughter round,
Nature's comedy, so profound.

Furry friends and leafy pals,
Share their secrets, giggles, and gales.
In this vault of green delight,
Every day is pure delight.

Chronicles of Endurance

In the grove, the branches hoot,
Tales of roots that take their loot.
A tale of strength with laughs around,
As hardwoods flex and sway unbound.

Wise stumps shout their victories,
Against the battle of the fees.
Who knew a tree could snicker so,
While knowing how far they will grow?

Mighty trunks with bark so thick,
Sharing jokes, a growing trick.
Through the storms and windy nights,
They stand proud, despite the fights.

When summer yields to autumn's chill,
They boast of the strength and will.
An epic found in every ring,
Nature's humor is the real king.

The Heart of the Woodland

A jolly bird begins to sing,
Inevitably, it starts to fling.
With wings a-flap, it brings the cheer,
As woodland friends all gather near.

A darting fox with much to say,
With twinkling eyes like a bright bouquet.
Cracking jokes from dusk till dawn,
The laughter echoes, never gone.

The heart of woods, with winks and quirks,
Each critter brimming with their perks.
Even shadows play mischievous parts,
In the dance of tickles and hearty hearts.

Oh, nature's humor, vast and grand,
Reveals itself in every strand.
A tapestry where giggles weave,
In the forest where we all believe.

Voices of the Evergreen

The whispers flow from twig to trunk,
As branches share their playful funk.
Evergreen laughter fills the air,
With secrets only trees would dare.

The pinecones drop, a clattering sound,
As laughter echoes all around.
Chipper chitter from squirrel to crow,
Nature's banter, a wondrous show.

The voices rise, a leafy choir,
Their rhymes and rhythms never tire.
Trees with jokes that twist and bend,
Forever sharing laughs, my friend.

In this forest of giggles and glee,
The woodland speaks with joyous decree.
Remember, amidst leaves so keen,
Laughter reigns in shades of green.

Odyssey of the Oldest

In a forest so lush, an old tree stood,
Telling jokes to the squirrels, oh, how they would!
With branches so wise, and leaves full of sass,
He tickled the birds as they flew by fast.

His bark told of tales from long, long ago,
Of acorns and storms, and the wild, wild show.
He chuckled at shadows that danced on the ground,
While the chipmunks chimed in with their laugh-out-loud sound.

With roots like a story that stretches so deep,
He'd slyly wink at the foxes who creep.
A bard in the woods, with humor so bright,
He filled the whole forest with joy and delight.

So here's to the old one, with jokes on the breeze,
Keeping secrets and laughter with such graceful ease.
In his leafy domains, life's never a bore,
With puns from the tree, who could ask for more!

Legends Woven in Wood

In the twilight's glow, a tale takes its flight,
Of a tree that could talk and dance through the night.
With a swish of his branches and a flash of his bark,
He'd start a wild party, igniting a spark.

The owls grooved softly with their wise little hoots,
While raccoons brought snacks in their fashionable suits.
Each laugh echoed over the shimmering brook,
As the fireflies twinkled, like stars in a book.

"Once upon a time," he said with a grin,
"Stop by for a story, pull up a branch, let's begin!
With legends of leaves and mishaps of vines,
I'll have you in stitches with these old punchlines!"

So whenever you wander through woods thick and wide,
Listen close to the whispers of laughter inside.
For tales full of fun and mischief abound,
In the heart of the forest, where joy can be found.

Heartbeat of the Forest

Deep in the woods, where the giggles grow loud,
Stands a tree living humor, a wonderful shroud.
His trunk is so thick, it wobbles with glee,
And the critters all chant, "He's the best—can't you see?"

"Hey, why did the beetle cross over the path?
To get to the joke that would make you just laugh!"
Everyone chuckled, from the ants to the deer,
As the tree told his stories, they gathered near.

With roots dancing wildly like ribbons of joy,
He tickled the ferns, and they shimmied like a toy.
"Life is a pun!" he'd declare in a roar,
As laughter rang out, echoing more and more.

So listen, dear friend, when you stroll through the trees,
The heartbeat of laughter floats on the soft breeze.
For nature's a stage where the fun never ends,
With trees full of humor and magical friends.

Mysteries of the Milieu

In the grove, a tree so spry,
Whispering secrets to the sky.
Its bark's got stories, quite a few,
Like a gossiping grandpa, it's true.

Leaves dance like they're on a spree,
With squirrels debating their next cup of tea.
One nutty rogue tried to climb up high,
But tumbled down, oh my, oh my!

Branches wave like they just don't care,
In a quirky contest for the air.
While birds compose their silly tunes,
The tree just chuckles 'neath the moon.

Roots stretch out, having a laugh,
Plotting pranks with every half,
A merry trickster in nature's realm,
The tallest joker at the helm.

Intertwined Lives

In the forest's embrace, they meet,
A tree and a squirrel, quite the feat.
"Shall I lend you a branch for your nest?"
"Only if you promise to host my guests!"

A raccoon arrives with a cheeky grin,
"Did you hear the joke about the wind?"
The tree just sways, "I'm quite a sound,
But you do know I can't spin around!"

Leaves giggle at tales of afternoon fun,
As the sun winks and the day is done.
An alliance forms both strong and sweet,
In the backyard stage where they all compete.

Together they stand, through thick and thin,
Sharing laughs in a world that's a win.
In this circus of life, they play their parts,
Intertwined are their wild little hearts.

Harbor of Hope

In the shade, a gathering place,
Where laughter echoes in endless space.
Friends come by, from far and wide,
For a chat under branches where joy resides.

A bird with a hat struts in style,
While a chubby rabbit lounges for a while.
"Have you heard the latest news, my friend?"
"It's about a cat who thinks she can blend!"

The tree leans in, with a twinkle of fun,
"Tell me more, oh won't this be a pun?"
As the critters share tales with squeaks and squeals,
The roots keep dancing, spinning their heels.

Even the shadows can't help but smile,
This harbor of hope has the best kind of style.
With each tale spun and laughter spread,
The tree chuckles softly, enough said!

Thunder and Tranquility

On a stormy day, branches sway,
A symphony plays, the clouds want to play.
Thunder rolls, a drum in the sky,
While leaves perform a wiggly fly.

"Don't worry, friends," the sturdy tree said,
"It's just nature's way of tapping her head."
Lightning twinkles like a cheeky grin,
While raindrops sing, "Let the fun begin!"

The critters huddle, cozy and snug,
Exchanging cozy tales, a heartwarming hug.
"Have you ever danced on a puddle or two?"
"It's a slippery sport, not for the faint, boo!"

After the storm, comes calm and cheer,
The tree wipes its branches, dries off a tear.
"Let's throw a party for all who stay,
To celebrate this wild, wacky day!"

Breath of the Earth

In the forest, a tree sings,
With bark like a clown's bright suit.
Branches sway, swing and fling,
Leaves giggle, oh what a hoot!

Critters gather, a lively crowd,
Squirrels joke, they can't be beat.
Swaying limbs make them so proud,
Who knew trees could dance on their feet?

Roots dig deep for a hearty laugh,
Tickling soil, they do their best.
Nature's jesters in green half,
Growing tall, forget the rest!

Sunshine sprinkles, warm and bright,
Each twig winks in all its glory.
Whispering tales of pure delight,
What a funny, greenish story!

Chronicle of the Change

Once upon a time, a sprout,
Stood up tall and made a scene.
With a wiggle and a shout,
It chatted all about its green bean.

Leaves turned red, then pink like pie,
Shaking off the winter's frown.
"I'm no more a simple guy,
Watch me twirl in autumn's crown!"

When summer came, the bugs did play,
Chomping leaves like it's their job.
But every munch was just okay,
'Cause they were wrapped in nature's mob.

In springtime, blooms had quite the flair,
Quirky colors all around.
With petals dancing in the air,
Chronicles of change are profound!

Harbinger of Harmony

In the grove, a playful breeze,
Turns branches into tiny drums.
Leaves clap hands with such great ease,
Nature's band, everybody hums!

Birds chirp jokes in happy tune,
Flapping wings like they're on stage.
Underneath the silver moon,
They're actors, turning every page!

Critters frolic, dance in glee,
Nuts bounce like jokes in the sun.
Together in their merry spree,
Life's comedy has just begun!

Harmony in every breath,
The forest laughs—oh, what a show!
Celebrating life, dodging death,
Musical moments steal the flow!

Dance of the Elements

A little gust sneezed, what a sight,
Puffed up leaves, they twirled and spun.
Raindrops giggled, oh what a fright,
Splashing puddles, oh, what fun!

Fireflies boogied in the night,
With little lights, they shone so bright.
Stars giggled, wishing in pure delight,
Earth's party didn't end till first light.

Across the sky, clouds did glide,
Each of them wore a fluffy hat.
They tickled the sun, oh, what pride,
Nature's dance, imagine that!

Elements joined for a joyful cheer,
In every corner, laughter and play.
Who knew they were such good peers,
In this world of funny array?

Guardians of the Earth

In a leafy hat, they stand so tall,
Guardians of nature, amusingly all.
With roots like a trampoline, they bounce around,
While critters below let out giggles, profound.

Their bark wears the scars of stories untold,
Like wise, old grandpas who love to be bold.
Branches wave wildly, a dance without care,
Squirrels and birds join in, none can compare.

Their shade offers laughter, where picnics unfold,
Some seek a muse in a story retold.
Planting themselves as the best of friends,
Together they thrive, where fun never ends.

So here's to the giants, in green and in brown,
Masters of mischief, that never wear frown.
Whispers of giggles rustle through leaves,
Guardians of laughter, nature's reprieves.

Through the Seasons' Lens

In springtime they shimmy, all dressed in their best,
Donning blossoms of pink, up close they impress.
But come summer's blaze, they change the routine,
Holding ice cream cones, living out our dream.

Autumn paints them in hues bright and spry,
Scattering laughter as leaves fly on high.
"Catch me if you can!" the branches now shout,
As squirrels do somersaults, giggles throughout.

Winter's a time for a cool game of freeze,
Jokes hidden beneath all those snowflakes with ease.
They wear coats of white, still full of delight,
"Who needs a snowman? We're trees of the night!"

Through seasons they play, a whimsical sight,
Guarding our joy with their zany delight.
Nature's own jesters, with spirits so bright,
Through the lens of time, they dance in the light.

Timeless Watcher

Standing like statues with wisdom so vast,
These sentinels chuckle, their memories cast.
With a bark full of jokes and leaves full of glee,
They watch every prank played by critters carefree.

The world keeps on spinning, but they never tire,
Witnessing all, from love to the fire.
"Did you see that leap?" their whispers all say,
As a rabbit forgets it's still April Fools' Day!

From roots deep in laughter to branches of cheer,
They've held every secret that time wants to hear.
A timeless observer in nature's embrace,
With a laugh and a wink, they keep up the pace.

So let's toast to the watchers, these trees of our days,
For their humor and wisdom in so many ways.
With each little chuckle that rustles the leaves,
A reminder that joy is what life achieves.

Cradle of Life

In the cradle of twigs where the wild ones chat,
A home for the critters, the great and the fat.
From mice to the owls, all gather around,
With laughter like music, a joyful sound.

Each party they throw has a feathery twist,
Inviting the windy breeze, who can't resist.
"Let's play hide and seek!" they shout with delight,
While shadows keep dancing throughout the night.

Nestled in branches, where giggles arise,
A cozy little nook under limitless skies.
Pinecone cupcakes topped with acorn sprinkles,
The feast is abundant, full of fun crinkles.

So here's to the cradle where life brings a cheer,
A tree-filled fiesta with friends far and near.
They're laughter's own home, as wild as can be,
Creating a world that's both funny and free.

Breath of the Wilderness

In the woods where squirrels play,
Branches dance the light away.
A tree so bold, it cracks a grin,
With bark like armor, ready to win.

Beneath the shade, the critters gather,
Whispers of the breeze, oh how they lather!
A lizard struts in stylish shoes,
While nearby rabbits share the news.

The sun dips low, the shadows prance,
Nature holds her wild romance.
Nearby a fox, in sneaky spree,
Steals a snack for a charming fee.

Giggles echo through the grove,
Every nook a tale to rove.
Laughter rings from leaf to root,
In this vibrant, joyful suit.

Hues of History

Once a sprout in a wildest dream,
Now a giant, a leafy scheme.
Stories whispered through the bark,
Each line a giggle, each ring a lark.

Chipmunks relish in the maze,
While owls chuckle through the haze.
Bugs parade in vibrant hues,
Setting the stage for nature's blues.

With every season comes a jest,
A drop of rain, a sunlit fest.
The old tree winks, it knows the game,
With every storm, a brighter claim.

Legends linger in its shade,
A tapestry of joys displayed.
In this vibrant family, wild and free,
Lies the history of you and me.

Echoes through the Vines

In the thicket where the laughter cracks,
Vines twist and turn, plotting their tracks.
A hummingbird with swagger flies,
Spins tales that can make you cry.

A raccoon with a top hat prances,
Conducting all the forest dances.
While butterflies in sequined wings,
Join the choir as nature sings.

From twisted roots to clover sprouts,
Voices tell of joyful bouts.
"Hey, watch this!" the crow does call,
As he tumbles down, a feathered fall.

Through laughter rings the twirling vines,
Life's a jest in nature's designs.
With every giggle, the world spins round,
In this echoing joy, pure love is found.

Tapestry of Twilight

As daylight dims and shadows blend,
The forest holds its myths to send.
Stars peek out with a cheeky wink,
While crickets chirp and pause to think.

The moon's a jester in the night,
Dancing clouds in soft candlelight.
Each rustle of leaves, a gentle tease,
As fireflies flicker, aiming to please.

A beaver in a bowtie stands,
Perfecting all his dam designs.
While owls hoot at passing fox,
Sharing tales from olden blocks.

As night unfolds its playful schemes,
Laughter mingles with sweet dreams.
In this tapestry of the dim-lit sky,
Nature's humor meets a joyful sigh.

The Strength of Stillness

In a forest, a tree, standing tall,
With a bark that could tell tales, after all.
Swaying lightly, not a bit shy,
Who knew a tree could fake a lullaby?

Chirping birds gather, ready to jive,
In the branches above, they feel so alive.
A squirrel sits snug, planning to dine,
On acorns that fell from its legume-gold shrine.

The wind teases leaves, starts a big fuss,
Yet the tree just chuckles, offers no fuss.
'I'm anchored right here', it whispers with glee,
'While you chase the breeze, just wait and see.'

Around it, the world spins fast, a wild race,
But it stands poised, with an elegant grace.
A sage in the woods, with wisdom to share,
Reminds us to pause, take in the fresh air.

Secrets Beneath the Bark

Beneath the tough shell, a party awaits,
With beetles and grubs, spinning lively plates.
They gnaw on the wood, living life without care,
Who knew the bark was a five-star affair?

Worms sneaking in, holding a dance,
With roots intertwined, they all take a chance.
'We're just hanging out,' they shout with a grin,
'Creating a ruckus deep under the skin!'

As the rains fall down and the sun gives a wink,
They chill beneath layers, sip sap and think.
In their wood-scented fiesta, no need for a chart,
They celebrate nature's own beat of the heart.

So if you hear chuckles from deep in the trunk,
Do not be surprised; it's just their own funk.
They've mastered the art of a hidden delight,
In the grand old tree, the fun's out of sight!

A Symphony of Seasons

Spring rushes in, like a child with a toy,
Blooming and buzzing, it brings so much joy.
Yet here in the canopy, the jokes never cease,
As blossoms confuse bees—like ants on a fleece!

Summer struts forth, with a sunbathing flair,
While squirrels all gather, doing summer hair.
One nutty old fellow falls right on his head,
He claims it's a badge—as they laugh and spread.

Fall brings a party, with leaves twirling down,
Pumpkins roll in, wearing grins, not a frown.
'Who tossed all this color?' asks a wise old crow,
While the branches erupt in a bright, merry show.

Winter arrives, all frosty and blue,
Blanketing the forest in silence anew.
But under the snow, the fun doesn't cease,
As a party of critters finds warmth and sweet peace.

The Embrace of Time

Once a small sprout, in the wide-open air,
It grows into legend—without a single care.
Each ring holds a story, a laugh and a tear,
Time tickles the bark, as it spins a tall leer.

With the seasons that change, the tree just winks,
'I'm here for the long haul, what do you think?'
When branches stretch wide and the sun starts to glare,
Mother Nature laughs, as she styles its hair.

Years roll along with a whimsical cheer,
A trunk that now carries the voices we hear.
With a twist and a turn, it dances so spry,
Proving age is just numbers on a cheeky pie!

In the end, it stands, proud as can be,
A comical heart, filled with timeless glee.
So let us remember, as life races fast,
To cherish the laughter, to make memories last!

Abode of the Wandering Spirits

In a forest where shadows chuckle,
Spirits sip tea in a real huddle,
A squirrel scolds them with a frown,
'Quit plotting mischief, you're not a clown!'

The owls roll their eyes in delight,
While raccoons plan heists at midnight,
A coyote joins in with a grin,
'What shenanigans can we begin?'

Branches sway with a playful dance,
As deer come by in a curious prance,
They peek at the spirits, wide-eyed and shy,
'You guys are weird, oh my, oh my!'

So if you wander deep through the trees,
Beware of the laughter carried by the breeze,
For here lies a realm of whimsical glee,
Where even the shadows want to be free!

Guardians of the Green

In the heart of the leaves, they assemble and scheme,
Tiny guardians whisper, fueling a dream,
A chipmunk declares, 'Let's have a race!'
While frogs ponder if they'll win first place!

A forgotten hat rests upon a stump,
The raccoon puts it on with a triumphant jump,
'Look at me! I'm the king of this glen!'
The others just laugh, 'Oh, not again!'

A wise old tree starts to chuckle and sway,
'You silly critters, you play all day,
Guardians we may be, but let's face the truth,
We're just a circus playing by youth!'

With twinkling eyes, they dance all the night,
Under a moon that's perfectly bright,
For in these woods, where the green does sigh,
Joy is the treasure that money can't buy!

Whispers of the Wild

In the stillness of dawn, the winds begin to tease,
'Who's making mischief among the tall trees?'
A fox whispers back, with a soft little laugh,
'Those raccoons again, plotting their path!'

The birds gossip loudly about last night's spree,
How the badgers discovered a stash of brie,
Laughter erupts, echoing far and wide,
The merry forest community swells with pride.

A wise old owl thinks he knows the score,
'These antics are fun, but I'm out the door,
I need my sleep before the sun climbs,
You rascals can play; I'm done with these rhymes!'

As sunlight peeks in, the whispers do fade,
But echoes of laughter in trees still cascade,
For nature holds secrets and giggles untold,
In the wild where joy is free and bold!

Chronicles of the Tree

Once upon a trunk, quite ancient and spry,
Lived a tree with a stash of old pie,
'Come one, come all, to the great tree feast!'
Squeaked a squirrel, striving to be the least!

The branches arched low for the critters in need,
While woodpeckers drummed out a merry beat,
A hedgehog arrives with a pizza so grand,
'What's the occasion? Is it all planned?'

But the tree just chuckled, 'It's just a surprise,
Every fallen branch tells tales in disguise,
So gather around, let's share in the cheer,
For we're all the stories that this bark holds dear!'

With laughter and snacks, they enjoyed through the night,
Creating a bond in the soft moonlight,
The chronicles of friends, forever alive,
In this place where joy and silliness thrive!

Keeper of Time

In the forest's green embrace,
Lies a tree with quite the face.
Its bark is thick, its leaves are wide,
Watch it sway, with so much pride.

Whispers tell of what it knows,
Secrets only nature shows.
It shimmies with a quiet glee,
A keeper of the time, you see!

With each tick of the sun's bright sphere,
It laughs away the passing year.
A barky grin, a twisty dance,
It makes the forest leap and prance!

So if you stop and lend an ear,
You might just hear it chuckle near.
The keeper clad in leafy guise,
With humor in its ancient eyes.

Jewel of the Woodland

Oh, jewel shining in the woods,
With branches dressed in leafy hoods.
A quirky tree, so proud and bright,
It tickles squirrels with delight.

Its gnarled limbs wave with flair,
At every passerby, they stare.
A comical twist, a friendly show,
'Tis hard to tell just where to go!

Beneath its shade, the creatures play,
From buzzing bees to deer at bay.
With laughter ringing through the air,
And nods from all who stop and stare.

Come and join this woodland spree,
With giggles shared 'neath the old tree.
A jewel so bright, it charms the day,
To chase your worries far away.

Lifeblood of the Valley

In a valley rich and wide,
A tree stands strong; it won't hide.
With roots that stretch and branches high,
It gives a wink as birds fly by.

Sipping sunlight, quenching thirst,
Though it seems it's always cursed.
For when the wind begins to howl,
It bends and sways, a trippy stroll!

From critters thousand, near and far,
It shares a laugh, a fond memoir.
A lifeblood flowing strong and true,
Yet still it plays peekaboo!

The valley sings, and so does she,
Her barky puns are the key.
The heart of all, with humor bold,
A life that never will grow old.

In the Heart of the Woods

In the heart of woods so grand,
Stands a tree, a jester planned.
Its trunk a pillar, proud and round,
With giggles swirling all around.

Each leaf a note, in breezy rhyme,
It dances to the tune of time.
With whispered jokes and playful breeze,
It turns the forest into a tease!

A riser of spirits, a comic sage,
On its wide branches, all engage.
Beneath its limbs, the laughter swells,
As nature spins its timeless bells.

So wander through this leafy maze,
And share in all its funny ways.
In the heart where joy is bred,
You'll find the puns that life has spread.

Reflections in the Bark

In the woods where critters cry,
Bizarre shapes dance and fly.
A squirrel in a top hat prances,
While the trees gossip in glances.

Bark that wrinkles like old skin,
Hides secrets deep within.
Woodpeckers laugh with silly taps,
Echoing the deer's mishaps.

Underneath, the mushrooms grow,
Wearing hats just like a show.
Each twisty root a tangled tale,
Of brave snakes who dared to scale.

Sunlight giggles, warms the floor,
All the leaves just beg for more.
As shadows dance in merry fray,
Joyful echoes rule the day.

Sanctuary of the Sunlight

In a glade where laughter rings,
Grasshoppers wear fancy bling.
Basking bugs unite for fun,
As butterflies race 'round the sun.

Branches stretch like arms in glee,
Inviting all for tea, you see.
A rabbit hops with a jaunty jig,
While a hedgehog plays the dig.

The sunlight drips like honey sweet,
Filling every nook and seat.
A dance of shadows starts to play,
As all the woodland critters sway.

Laughter echoes, fills the air,
Nature's jesters, everywhere.
In this haven, pure delight,
Every day is a silly flight.

Keepers of the Whispering Woods

In the trees, a council meets,
Where the wise old owl tweets.
Chirping birds cast humorous bets,
On who'll win the dance-off sets.

Frogs in ties hop to and fro,
Debating who should run the show.
While ants in suits march in line,
Planning feasts with grand design.

With each rustle, laughter spills,
As the wind grins through the hills.
Tales of sly foxes fill the night,
In this woodland, pure delight.

The trees lean in to catch the jest,
Nature's whimsy at its best.
A riot of sound in the green,
In the woods, life's a fun routine!

Portrait of Persistence

A trunk that twists and turns with cheer,
Mocks the storms it laughs at sheer.
Roots dig in, a determined dance,
While critters pause to steal a glance.

With every season, colors change,
Surprises lurk, it's rather strange.
While time cheers on with a hearty clap,
Resilience wears a charming cap.

Bouncing back from every whack,
This sturdy stem won't fade to black.
Leaves wear smiles, a vibrant hue,
Swaying proudly, brave and true.

In the face of every trial,
It shakes its limbs with cheeky style.
A testament to life's embrace,
In this dance, we find our place.

Secrets Buried Beneath

In the shade where whispers dwell,
Beneath a trunk that knows too well.
Squirrels gossip, stealing acorns,
Secrets shared till the dawn is borne.

Roots are tangled like a knot,
Finding treasures, oh what a lot!
Hidden snacks and lost shoes too,
Nature's humor in a view.

Boughs and Blossoms

Up above the frolicsome birds,
Chirping tales without any words.
A branch dips low for a friendly chat,
While bees buzz gossip, imagine that!

Petals dance like a silly clown,
Wearing pollen as their crown.
Laughter echoes on the breeze,
Nature's fun in the rustling leaves.

Echoes of the Seasons

Winter's joke, a blanket of white,
Snowflakes falling in a frosty flight.
Spring comes bouncing, a green parade,
Flowers trickling, like they've made a trade.

Summer swings on a sunlit beam,
Ice cream spills, what a crazy dream!
Autumn chuckles with leaves that twirl,
A riot of color in a whirling swirl.

Tides of Time

Time's a jester, a cheeky sprite,
Hiding treasures in the moonlight.
Each year a giggle, each month a grin,
With stories that tickle from deep within.

We swing from branches, we sway and leap,
In laughter's grasp, a joy to keep.
So plant those roots and let love grow,
In the mighty line where the breezes blow.

Sun-Kissed Resilience

In a forest where tall trees sway,
A bushy friend likes to play.
With bark so smooth, it gleams with cheer,
It waves its branches, drawing near.

When sunbeams tickle its leafy crown,
It laughs and twirls while upside down.
With roots so deep, it stands so proud,
Making all the other trees feel cowed.

In winter's chill, with snowflakes laugh,
It swaggers on, a daring half.
Joking that it's just dressed for style,
"Let's dance!" it shouts, with a wink and smile!

So here's to the one who takes a chance,
With quips and jests, it leads the dance.
In sunshine's glow or moonlight's thrall,
That quirky soul inspires us all.

In The Shadow of Giants

Amidst the titans reaching high,
A little sprout gives a cheeky sigh.
"Why so serious, you towering crew?
Join me for fun, it's long overdue!"

With limbs extended like a bright parade,
It teases the oaks, "You're all just shade!"
With humor sharp and giggles loud,
It steals the spotlight, brave and proud.

"Come play a game! It's called 'Who's Tall?'
But I've got stretches—not so small!"
The giants chuckle, roots intertwined,
"Your spirit's bright, you're one of a kind!"

In this wild grove where laughter reigns,
The small play tricks on the great with gains.
So raise a toast to the sprightly sprite,
For with every jest, it lights up the night!

Beneath the Cascading Sky

On a breezy day, just look around,
A whimsical sprite is joyfully found.
With a grin so wide, it greets the sun,
"Come have some fun, let's play, let's run!"

With clouds as cushions, it bounces high,
Crafting jokes that float on by.
"Why did the woodpecker blush so red?
I think it heard you talking 'head'!"

As raindrops dance on this lively scene,
It cracks a smile, "I'm a water machine!"
Chasing drops that plink and plop,
This merry soul just can't stop!

So let the winds carry tales of glee,
Where laughter flows like a vibrant sea.
Under the arches of blue so wide,
It finds joy, where dreams reside!

An Invitation to Reverie

Join me, friends, for a playful flight,
In dreamlands full of sheer delight.
Where trees share secrets with sparkling air,
And tickle each other without a care!

With smiles that stretch like cozy vines,
They gather to share their grand designs.
"Let's tell a story of how we grew,
And sprinkle some giggles, just for you!"

Beneath golden beams and cheerful shouts,
Everyone smiles and hops about.
"Here's to the quirky, the wacky, the wise,
We're all just trees wearing silly ties!"

So come along, let's set the pace,
With laughter echoing through every space.
An invitation to a dream-filled day,
Where loving nature comes out to play!

Roots Reaching Deep

In a forest green, roots like fingers,
They tickle the ground, just like singers.
With a wiggle and shake, they dance in the dirt,
Who knew that undergrounds could be so alert?

Through twirls and spins, they map out a tale,
Of mismatched socks and a squirrel on a trail.
They whisper to rocks, give a shout to a gopher,
A root-ritual, where each day is a roper!

With some light-hearted pranks, they tug on the soil,
As the wind blows softly, like they're in a coil.
A comedy troupe in a leafy abode,
Life can be funny on this twisting road.

With laughter and glee, they tickle the breeze,
Creating a ruckus, as happy as you please.
Roots reaching out with a boisterous call,
In the grand game of life, they're the life of the ball!

Legacy of the Leaves

Once green and bright, but now they've all tricked,
Flipping into autumn, they've cleverly picked.
A fashion show on branches, a colorful spree,
Who knew that leaves could have such comedy?

They flutter and flounce like the latest craze,
Whirling in circles, a leaf-choreographed phase.
With a dance in the air, they twirl and they spin,
Next thing you know, they've grabbed a good grin!

From lofty high tops to the ground they do drop,
Each rustle and tumble, a giggling bop.
Their legacy's laughter, always in reach,
When leaves play the game, they always can teach!

So gather your joy, let the leaves take you high,
With chuckles and jests, they whisper and sigh.
A legacy spun from each fluttering way,
Leaves cracking up, come see their display!

Arbor's Embrace

Embraced by the winds in a hug oh so tight,
Branches are jesters, what a comical sight!
Swaying and laughing, under skies bright,
They tip their hats to the day and the night.

With knots in their limbs, they bow to the floor,
Sharing their wisdom like never before.
Got jokes in their bark and puns in their shade,
Every whiff of the breeze, a giggly tirade.

Branches like dancers with moves so absurd,
Swinging and swooping, without a word.
What fun to be wrapped in a tree's gentle grin,
In the embrace of the wild, let the fun begin!

So climb up, be merry, let cheer take its place,
For the humor of trees is a glorious grace.
Under the arbor, find solace and play,
In this leafy embrace, laugh your worries away!

Harmony Within the Hues

In a palette of greens, yellow, and brown,
A funny old willow sat wearing a crown.
He painted the world with a splash of the sun,
And said, "Life is better when we're all having fun!"

The reds sing a song, the blues join the dance,
Together they kick up a whimsical prance.
With giggles and grins that float through the air,
Each hue holds a secret, a colorful flair.

From chartreuse to russet, they all work in sync,
Creating a canvas where joy's at the brink.
They chuckle and joke, creating a tune,
Nature's own symphony beneath the bright moon.

So look all around at the colors so bright,
In harmony's arms, find yourself in delight.
Together they flourish, a fantastic crew,
A riot of laughter in every hue!

Reflections Under the Sun

The branches wave like dancers in glee,
As squirrels debate on what should be free.
Sunlight giggles on leaves so bright,
While shadows play hide and seek in delight.

Birds hold court on the highest limb,
Bickering over a snack that's quite slim.
The laughter of nature, a charming display,
Bet you could join in if only you'd stay!

Songbird's Sanctuary

A feathered choir sings tunes to the sky,
While robins in tuxedos all bob and fly.
Each whistle a joke, a punchline well-timed,
You'd think they rehearsed, everything well rhymed!

Nestled atop, the best of the best,
Exchanging their secrets, a funny old jest.
With chirps and with fluffs, they claim their own stage,
In this leafy retreat, the laughter won't age!

Vows of the Earth

Two ants waltz together, a miniature dance,
While crickets debate if it's science or chance.
The soil chuckles, tickled by feet,
As worms wiggle forth, don't miss the great beat!

Each blade of grass sways to the tune,
Whispering gossip beneath the bright moon.
The roots tie their bonds, as they weave and they spark,
A promise made here, with laughter and lark!

Illumination in the Shade

Under the canopy, a world of delight,
A picnic of shadows, a whimsical sight.
With ants carrying crumbs from the feast,
The wind tells a story, like a bard at least!

Through dappled light, giggles sparkle and flare,
A raccoon peeks out, with a mischievous stare.
With grins and with nudges, they plot and they play,
In this realm of the quirky, the fun leads the way!

Shade of the Forgotten

In a forest thick with chatter,
A tree wears glasses, oh what a patter!
Leaves like laughter, tickling the air,
With squirrels debate, is it really fair?

It sways with glee in a gentle breeze,
While branches dance like uncles at ease.
Its roots tell tales of long-lost socks,
And whispers secrets of wooden clocks.

When birds come to rest, they bring their jokes,
A stand-up show, they're feathered folks!
They croon and cackle, compete for the crown,
While the tree just chuckles, never a frown.

In twilight glow, it stretches wide,
A hammock for dreams, where giggles reside.
So grab a seat, forget your woes,
Under this shade, life's a grandiose show!

Echoes of the Evergreen

Amongst the pines, a voice rings clear,
A cheeky echo, loud and near.
It mocks the heights, with a playful shout,
"Look at me, all dressed in sprout!"

The trees all giggle, their needles shake,
As the echo teases, a comical flake.
With every bounce off bark and bough,
Laughter ripples, "Can you top this somehow?"

In the dance of the wind, it spins a tale,
Of a pinecone prince who promised to sail.
But tangled in branches, he took a spill,
Now he shares punchlines on every hill.

As the moon sneaks in for a soft, sweet glow,
The trees trade jokes, putting on a show.
In whispers and giggles, they laugh with delight,
For echoes of joy fill the starry night!

Embrace of the Earth

A root wraps tight around a stray shoe,
Fashion statement? It's hard to construe.
Firm in the soil, the tree takes pride,
In footwear fashion, it won't be denied!

With worms as stylists, they wiggle and squirm,
Giving each branch some unique form.
"Watch and learn!" chirps a wise old toad,
As he croaks out jokes, striking a pose!

The flowers have shades, a colorful crew,
Whispering secrets in morning dew.
They chat about blossoms, spread bright and wide,
With petals like feathers, they flaunt with pride.

When rain starts to dance, the mud gets all slick,
The roots play hopscotch, a humorous trick.
With giggles and splashes, the joy takes din,
Embraced by the earth, where the laughter begins!

Song of the Verdant Leaves

In a leafy grove, a band takes flight,
With drums of acorns, they groove all night.
The leaves rustle softly, a harmony sweet,
As nature's musicians tap their feet.

A mischievous breeze joins the beat,
And sways the branches; it can't be beat!
With every rustle a punchline's served,
The orchestra chuckles, entirely swerved.

Frogs croon a tune, while crickets play bass,
Even a snail joins with unhurried grace.
Side-splitting laughter fills the air with zest,
As forest critters compete for the best!

Under the starlight, the concert goes on,
With each cozy note, all worries are gone.
So dance in the shadows, keep spirits high,
In the song of the leaves, let your laughter fly!

Branches of Hope

In a forest so grand, a tree stood tall,
With branches that waved like they were at a ball.
Squirrels held parties, they danced in the breeze,
While birds took their turns to strut with such ease.

Some folks called it a prank, that tree full of cheer,
It tickled the sun with its foliage sheer.
Underneath it, the critters shared secrets of old,
While laughing at shadows that dared be so bold.

The trunk had a twist, it looked kind of shy,
But whispered sweet jokes as the clouds drifted by.
Beneath its wide skirt, the laughter would swell,
And even the gnomes would break into a yell!

Branches adorned with a whimsy delight,
Each leaf like a jester, dressed up for the night.
So if you're nearby, join in and partake,
For joy is contagious, make no mistake!

Ancestral Arms

Twisted and gnarled, a family tree,
With branches like arms that hug you with glee.
It holds ancient tales, like a grandparent's grin,
With every new ring, it says, "Let's begin!"

Amongst all those limbs, a wise owl speaks clear,
"Don't take life too serious, just laugh, my dear!"
With a wink and a hoot, it gives folks a nudge,
To dance with the wind, and not hold a grudge.

The knots tell a story of whimsical strife,
Of squirrels on quests for the ultimate life.
"No acorn left behind!" the slogans declare,
As they plot and they scheme without worldly care.

Beneath the great canopy, friendships are bound,
Where even the lost souls feel welcome and found.
With its arms open wide, it whispers, "Just be,
For life's but a giggle in this tall, leafy spree!"

Dance of the Dryads

When the evening sun dips, they gather with flair,
The dryads arrive with light-footed care.
With twirls and with shimmies, they liven the night,
Playing leapfrog with shadows in pure delight.

They tug at the branches, a mischievous team,
And sway with the whispers of an alpha dream.
Under the moon, their laughter takes flight,
As fireflies twinkle, sharing the light.

Each step in the grass is a giggle revealed,
Reflections of joy that seemed long concealed.
Braiding the breezes, weaving the trees,
This merry band of spirits dances with ease.

Lifting their voices, harmonies soar,
The grand tree sways gently, begging for more.
With roots deep in fun, they twine and they play,
In the heart of the night, they dance till the day!

Love Letters to the Cloud

A tree whispers softly to bright puffs above,
"Oh, lofty companion, you fit me like a glove!"
With each passing breeze, it sends up a note,
A flutter of feelings in a leaf-shaped boat.

"You make me feel fluffy, bring rain just for free,
I'm rooted and crazy, like a wild jubilee!"
The clouds giggle back with a thunderous cheer,
As they bump and they jostle, spreading joy here.

With misty embraces, they share in delight,
While the weather forecasts are slathered in light.
Each drop of affection, a playful remark,
As the tree shakes its leaves under the spark.

"Let's create a storm, make the squirrels cavort,
In a game of tag, don't sell us short!"
They giggle and stretch, both clad in nature's charm,
A love story written in wind and in calm.

www.ingramcontent.com/pod-product-compliance
Lightning Source LLC
Chambersburg PA
CBHW071830160426
43209CB00003B/262